This book is dedicated to my parents and grandparents, who put a love for the mountains and a good pancake deep in my soul.

THE GRANDS GO... OH NO!

THE GREAT SMOKY MOUNTAINS

THE GRANDS GO - OH NO!
The Smoky Mountains

Text Copyright©2021 A.N. Eason
ISBN 978-1-7365753-0-7 paperback
ISBN 978-1-7365753-1-4 hardback
Library of Congress Control Number 2006907531

All rights reserved. This book may not be reproduced in whole or in part in any form, or by any means, without express written permission from the publisher.

Published by:
Reason Publishing
reasonpublishing@gmail.com

Illustrations by Toby Mikle

For information: www.grandsgo.com

Written By A.N. Eason
Illustrated by Toby Mikle

This book belongs to:

MOMANDAXON
_____

Anytime I go with the Grands,
I know they've made a whole lot of plans!

Lots of new things are on the list,

Like magical mountains covered in mist;

Rivers with rocks to climb all around,

Looking for salamanders -
red, green, and brown;

Pancakes shaped like bears in snow,

And tubing down a river slow;

A park with rides to suit us all,

Made by a lady whose hair is tall.

The plans are set,
So off we go,

But....

My stomach is rolling all topsy-turvy.

We stop beside a cool mountain stream;

Continuing on and driving with care,
The cars suddenly stop -

We see a bear!

A mama bear leading three cubs in a row,

Crosses in front of us, cautious and slow.

"We wouldn't have seen this without stopping a while!"

We finish our trip, leaving some things undone,
But The Grands say that is what makes it so fun!

Traveling together never goes quite as planned,
Whether cities or parks, mountains or sand.

But we keep this in mind, this one thing we know,
Spending time with each other is the reason we go.

Trip Journal

Date _____

Who went

_____

_____

_____

Favorite Memory

_____

_____

_____

For Trip Suggestions and Playlist
go to
www.grandsgo.com

Made in the USA
Monee, IL
07 September 2021